**special introduction and summary
by Chris Spencer**

© 1980 David C. Cook Publishing Co.
850 N. Grove Ave.
Elgin, IL 60120
All rights reserved
ISBN: 0-89191-283-5

Published 1980 by World Distributors (Manchester) Limited
A Member of The Pentos Group
PO Box 111, 12 Lever Street, Manchester M60 1TS
Designed and produced for World Distributors (Manchester) Limited by
Asset Publishing Limited
Copyright © 1980 Asset Publishing Limited
Printed in Italy

The Stories Jesus Told
The Good Shepherd

written by Heather Dyer
illustrated by Bernard Brett

Jesus was a wonderful storyteller, as you will see if you read through the Gospels — the first four books of the New Testament. But his stories, which are called parables, were not told just for people to listen to and enjoy. There were deeper meanings to them, and lessons to be learned from each one. Through his parables — and through his whole teaching — Jesus was showing us what God is like and how important it is for us to trust God and to follow the example Jesus was setting for us.

In his parables Jesus always talked about things that anyone could understand—the things everyone would find around them. He spoke of sheep, farms, fish, seeds, bread, fruit, money, to mention but a few. And when he told his parables everyone listened, for he spoke in a way that brought alive the teaching church leaders made stuffy and boring. Jesus often had harsh words to say to these men because many of them thought they were better than everyone else. You can read about how he did this in some of the parables in this series.

ONCE there was a shepherd who had a hundred sheep. This man was wise and kind and took great care of his flock. Every morning he would take them to the hills where they would eat the fresh, green grass. When the sun got hot, he would find a stream or a pool of water where they could drink.

The sheep were fond of the shepherd, too, and when he called them they would follow him. In spring some of the ewes in the flock had baby lambs. They were full of fun and would skip about and play games with each other. Sometimes they would stray away from the flock. Then their mothers would call them back, and the old shepherd would pick up the very small ones and carry them back in his arms if their wobbly legs were tired.

Every evening, before darkness came, the shepherd would call his flock together and take them to the sheepfold where they would spend the night. The sheepfold was like a little round house without a roof. It was built of stones and had high walls and a small space for the door. The walls were high to stop wild animals getting in, for many creatures prowled around at night looking for a lamb for their supper. But the shepherd knew the sheep would be safe inside the sheepfold. He would lie down in the space where the door would have been so that he could fight off any animals that might try to get in.

One day the shepherd took his sheep to a hill where the sheep had not been before. They liked that. They nosed about as they nibbled at the grass, and some of them went exploring. It was a lovely day in early summer, and the fields were covered with daisies and

other flowers. Up in the blue sky the larks were singing, and bees hummed busily among the flowers. The shepherd had been playing a tune on his reed pipe, but now he was tired. His head began to nod in the hot sun, and very soon he fell fast asleep.

Now in the flock there was one little lamb who was always looking for new places to visit and new things to do. While the shepherd was asleep and his mother was busy eating, the little lamb decided to explore the other side of the hill. It was rocky there, with thornbushes among the grass, and he had a lovely time chasing the little blue butterflies and making friends with the rabbits. He was running races with one of the rabbits when all of a sudden he slipped and fell down a rocky ledge right into the middle of a thornbush. He tried to get up, but the rock was steep and the thorns caught in his wool. The little lamb cried and called for his mother. But she was much too far away to hear him, and the shepherd had not even noticed he was gone.

Evening came, and as the sun began to sink and the dark shadows appeared, the little lamb was very frightened. Suppose a lion found him? Oh, if only he had stayed with his mother!

Back on the other side of the hill, the shepherd called his sheep together and led them slowly back to the sheepfold. He stood in the doorway as he always did and counted the sheep as they went in. One, two, three, four.... But when he came to ninety-nine, he stopped. There was one missing. The shepherd was very worried. He counted again to make quite sure, but there were only ninety-nine.

"Whatever shall I do?" he said. "One of them must have strayed while I was asleep. I must go and look for it."

So he told one of the boys to look after the rest of the sheep while he was gone, and went back to the hill where they had been that day. He looked everywhere, but the little lamb was nowhere to be seen.

"Perhaps it has strayed into another flock," the shepherd said to himself. "I must visit the other sheepfolds and ask the shepherds if they have an extra sheep in their flock tonight."

He climbed the hill to the first sheepfold. The shepherd there was warming himself by the side of a bonfire he had lit to keep the wild animals away, for they do not like fire. The twigs snapped and crackled in the hot flames, and the shepherd held out his hands in front of the warm blaze.

"Did you find an extra sheep in your flock tonight?" he asked. The other shepherd shook his head.

"No," he said. "I'm sorry if you have lost one." He knew how worried the shepherd must be. A sheep alone at night on the hillside could be a meal for a wild animal.

The shepherd pulled his cloak around him. The night was cold now, and he looked longingly at the warm fire. But there were other sheepfolds he must visit.

One by one he visited the other shepherds, and one by one they each shook their heads. None of them had found his little lost lamb.

The shepherd knew the only thing left for him to do was to wander over all the hillsides in search of his lost lamb. He took his heavy stick just in case he should meet a lion or one of the bears that lived in the caves in that area.

He searched and searched, calling its name. The little lamb heard him, but of course it could not come to the shepherd because it was stuck in the thornbush. Its voice was so weak from bleating that it could hardly utter a sound. It called in a little croaky voice.

The shepherd stopped and listened. Was that a lamb's cry? He made his way through the rocks and bushes in the direction the sound came from. Peering through the darkness, he could just see the little lamb caught in the bush. Gently he moved away the prickles, picked up the little lamb, and held it in his arms.

"You poor little thing," he said, softly stroking its little pink nose. "We will soon have you home, and then I'll put oil on your cuts and make them better. Now I must go and tell the other shepherds that you have been found."

The little lamb nestled up against the man's rough

cloak. He was so happy to be found. The shepherd was happy, too; in fact so happy that he forgot how tired he was as he visited all his friends.

"I've found my little lost lamb," he told each one in turn. "I'm so happy." The shepherds nodded as they sat by their fires, and they were happy, too.

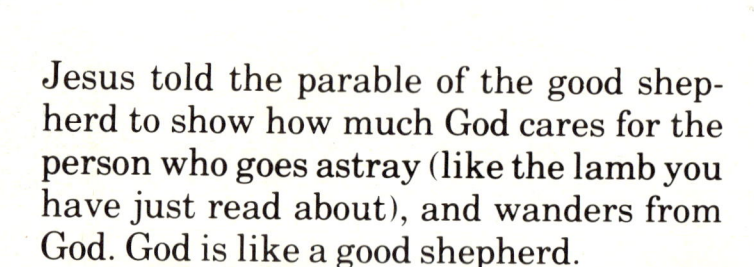

Jesus told the parable of the good shepherd to show how much God cares for the person who goes astray (like the lamb you have just read about), and wanders from God. God is like a good shepherd.

Other writers in the Bible used the idea of men being like sheep. In the Old Testament the prophet Isaiah says that "we have strayed away like sheep; we have left God's paths to follow our own." This picture would have been easily understood by the people Jesus was talking to, for many of them were shepherds or worked with sheep in some other way.

In this parable Jesus is saying that God loves each of us just as the shepherd loves his sheep. He does not always wait for the person who has wandered to return to him, but goes out searching for the "lost sheep" and doesn't give up until he is found.